The Military

on the MAP

Alix Wood

PowerKiDS press

New York

Published in 2015 by Rosen Publishing
29 East 21st Street, New York, NY 10010

Copyright © 2015 by the Rosen Publishing Group, Inc.
Produced for Rosen by Alix Wood Books

Editor for Alix Wood Books: Eloise Macgregor
Designer: Alix Wood
US Editor: Joshua Shadowens
Researcher: Kevin Wood
Geography Consultant: Kerry Shepheard, B.Ed (Hons) Geography

Photo Credits: Cover, 2, 4 middle, 5, 6, 7 e, f, g, h, and j, 8, 9, 11, 12, 13, 14 middle
and bottom, 15 bottom, 16, 18, 19 main and bottom, 22, 23, 26 top © Shutterstock;
1, 4 top and bottom, 7 a, b, c, d, and j, 10, 15 middle, 19 top, 21, 24 inset,
26 bottom left and right, 28, 29 © DoD; 14 top © Mr Armstrong2

Publisher's Cataloging Data

Wood, Alix.
The military on the map / by Alix Wood.
p. cm. — (Fun with map skills)
Includes index.
ISBN 978-1-4777-6968-3 (library binding) — ISBN 978-1-4777-6969-0 (pbk.) —
ISBN 978-1-4777-6970-6 (6-pack)
1. United States—Armed Forces —Juvenile literature. 2. Navigation—History—
Juvenile literature. 3. Maps—Juvenile literature. I. Wood, Alix. II. Title.
UA23.W69 2015
910.4—d23

Manufactured in the United States of America

CPSIA Compliance Information: Batch #WS14PK9: For Further Information contact Rosen Publishing, New York, New York at 1-800-237-9932

Contents

Military Maps

The military is a country's armed forces. The military need to be good at reading maps. They have to know where they are, and where their enemy is. A map is a diagram of the Earth's surface. Maps can be of a large area such as a country, or a small area such as an army base. It would be difficult to show someone where something was without a map. Maps help you to go in the right direction.

▲ An army soldier writes down map directions while on patrol in Afghanistan.

No one type of map or globe can show the military everything they need to know. They use several different kinds of maps. A globe is a map shaped like a ball. Because it is almost the same shape as the Earth, a globe can show exactly how the Earth looks. It can't show much detail, though. Sometimes the military need to see a close-up view of an area.

Do You Know?

This radar screen shows how the military use radar maps to scan the airspace for aircraft. The white line shows the direction the antenna is pointing as it sweeps around.

► A radar antenna

Maps are usually flat. Maps can show close-up detail. They can fold and go in your pocket, too. Soldiers couldn't really carry large globes around with them on patrol! People who make maps have to turn the curved Earth's surface into a flat drawing. These types of maps are called **projections**. Projections alter the shape of the continents. Can you find out what's wrong with Greenland and Australia in the map below?

▶ This map is made using the Mercator projection. It is drawn as though a sheet of paper had been wrapped around the globe. The areas around the middle are accurate, but the areas to the top and bottom of the map are distorted.

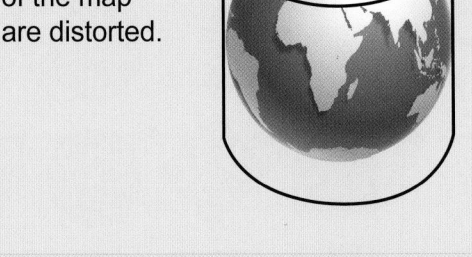

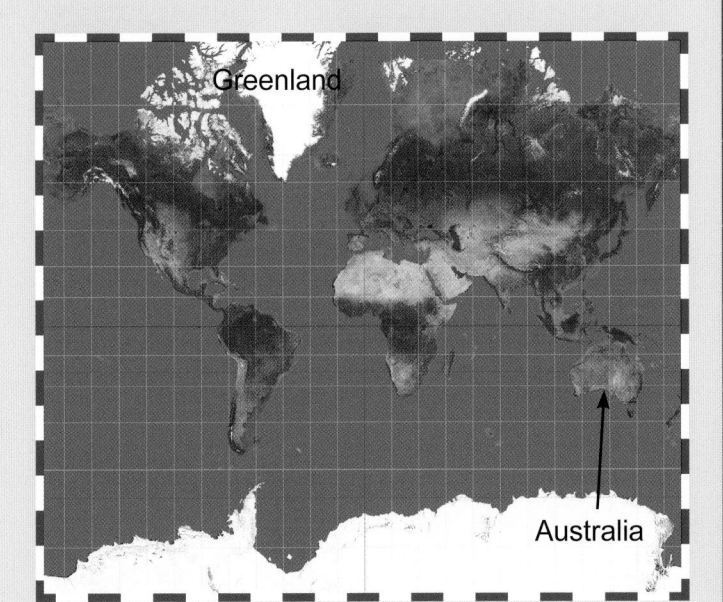

The Trouble With Flat Maps...

Flat maps change the shape and relative size of some areas. The Mercator projection above shows Greenland as larger than Australia. Australia is really over three and a half times larger than Greenland!

The military use flat maps which use a Mercator projection. To make it accurate, they use a special grid system to pinpoint places on the map. They also use close-up satellite images which show a real view of the Earth.

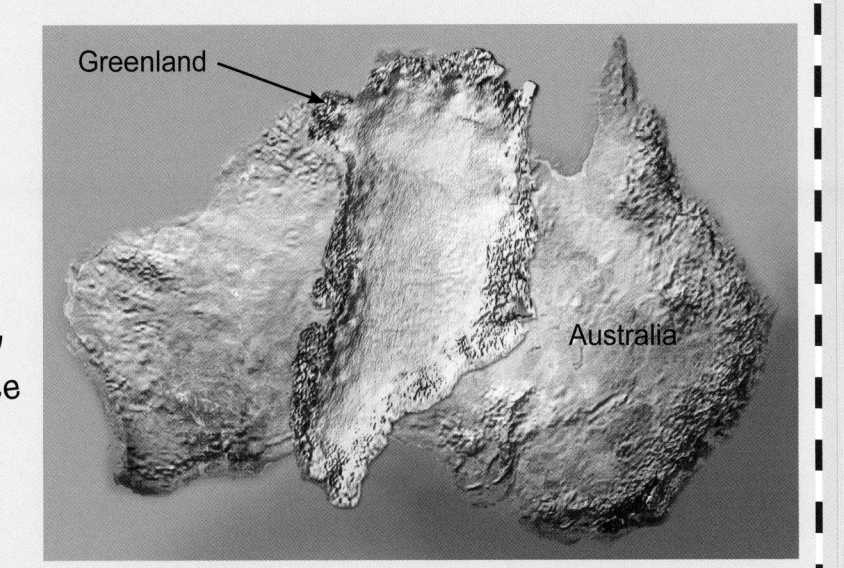

Using Symbols

Maps often use pictures instead of words to show where things are. These pictures are called symbols. Symbols are very important on military maps. An organization called NATO was formed after World War II. The countries that belong to NATO work together to defend themselves and each other. The member countries speak many different languages. Their maps need to be clear and use symbols that any language can understand.

Symbols need to be clear and simple. These NATO symbols use the colors blue, green, red, and yellow to label friendly, neutral, enemy, and unknown objects on a map. Neutral means that the object is neither friendly nor an enemy. Because the symbols might have to be understood in bad light they also have different shapes.

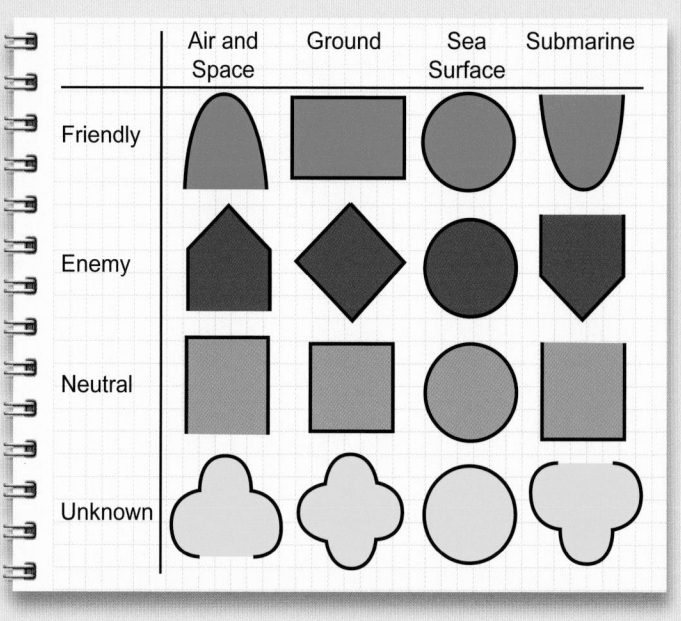

	Air and Space	Ground	Sea Surface	Submarine
Friendly				
Enemy				
Neutral				
Unknown				

🔍 Try Your Skills

Can you count how many of the following are on this map? Use the table above to help you.

1. Enemy submarines
2. Friendly ships
3. Unknown aircraft
4. Neutral ground forces

6

Symbols Matching Game

A key usually shows you what the symbols on a map stand for. Symbols have to be very simple drawings as they need to be small on maps.

See if you can label this key by matching each symbol with the right photograph.

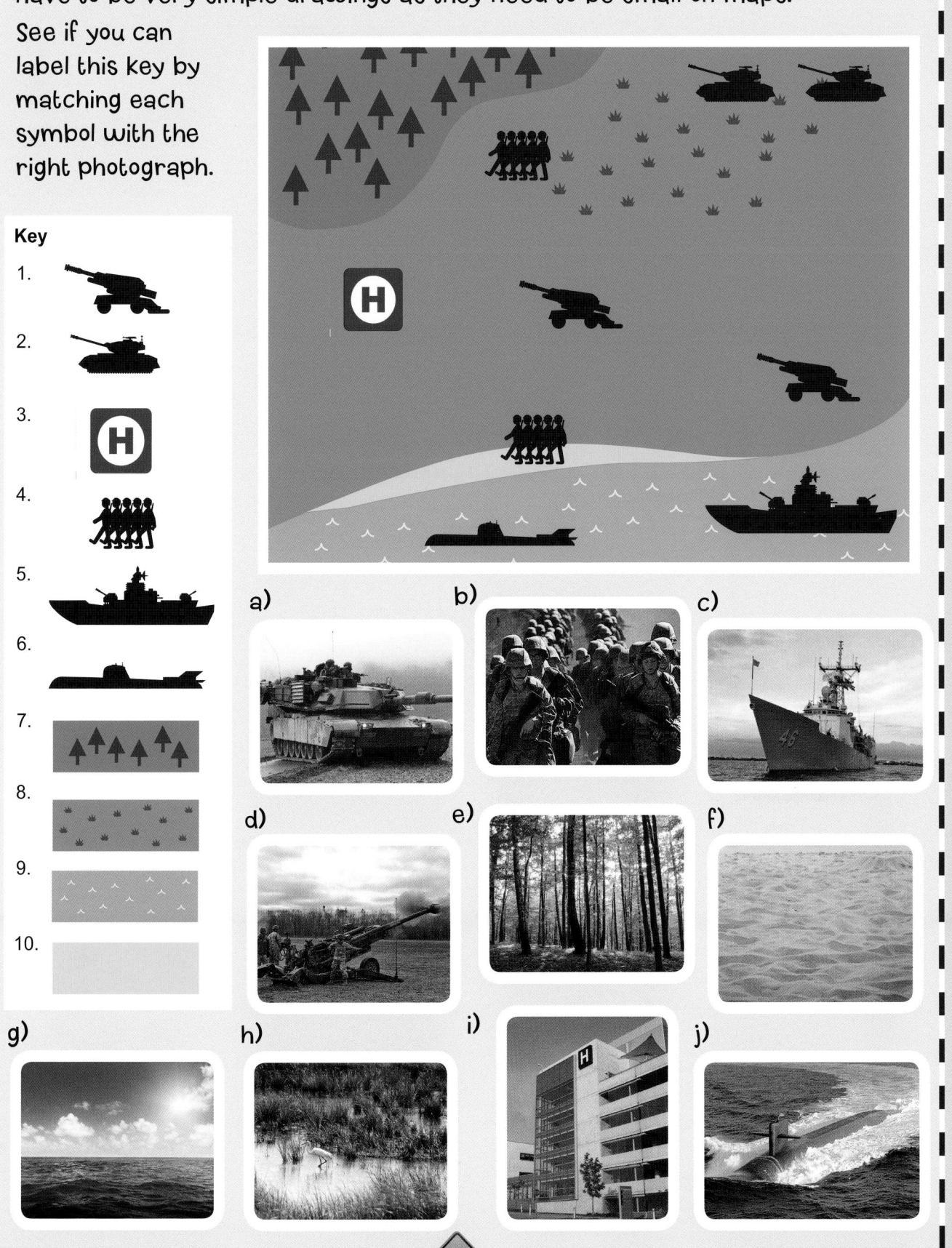

Key

1.
2.
3.
4.
5.
6.
7.
8.
9.
10.

a)

b)

c)

d)

e)

f)

g)

h)

i)

j)

Using a Compass

The Earth is like a giant magnet. The north and south poles are magnetic. A compass has a magnetic needle which will always point to the **north magnetic pole**. The **compass rose** shows the points of the compass. The four main **cardinal directions** are north, south, east, and west.

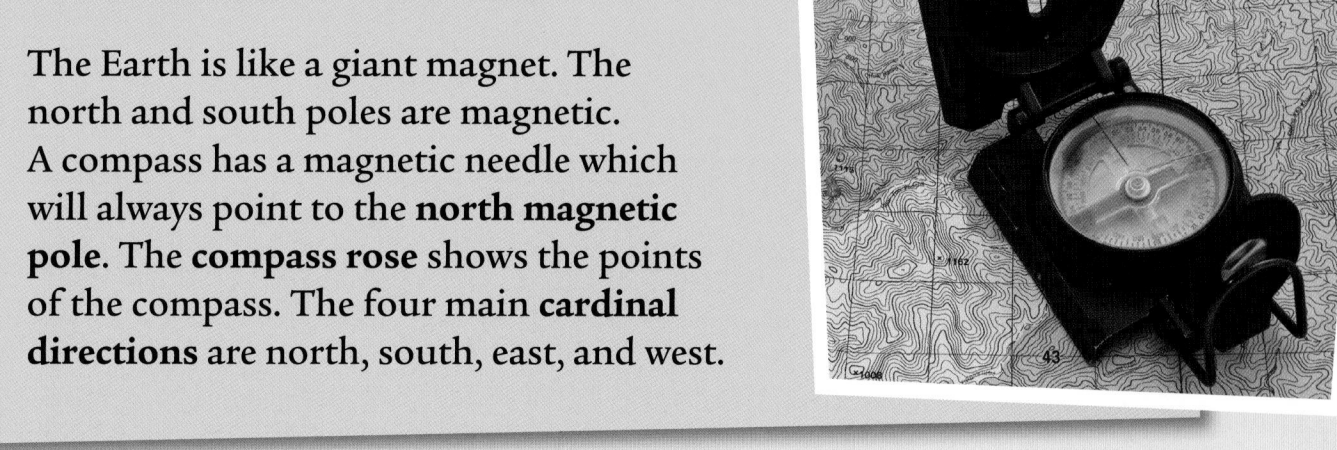

Maps will usually have a drawing of a compass rose on them. On most maps north points toward the top of the map. If you go clockwise around the compass the main points are north, then east, then south, and finally west. They are usually written using just their first letter, N, E, S, and W. The circle on a compass is divided into 360 degrees. Compass points are sometimes known by their degrees. For example east is also 90°.

Try Your Skills

Can you work out which compass points are at

1. 180°?
2. 270°?
3. 0°?
4. Which compass point could also be called 360°?

Do You Know?

An easy way to remember the points of the compass is to say this phrase: **Never Eat Soggy Waffles.**

North, South, East, or West?

Accurate compass directions are essential for hitting enemy targets. Help these special forces reach their targets. Use the compass to help you.

PYLON ISLAND

SENTRY BOX

SOLAR PANELS

Your Mission

Your helicopter has landed on an enemy island.

1. Run for cover in the mountains. In what direction should you head?
2. From the mountain, what direction in degrees do you need to head to the sentry box?
3. From the sentry box, what direction should you head to attack Pylon Island?
4. From the sentry box, what direction should you go to attack the solar panels?
5. Which way do you need to head to get back to the helicopter from the solar panels?

Maps With Grids

A grid divides a map into squares. You can tell someone exactly what square an object is in by using the numbers or letters written along the edges. To write a **grid reference**, write down the number that goes along the grid first. Then write the number that goes up and down. You can remember the order by saying "go along the corridor and then up the stairs."

This is a plan of an army base. You can direct people to places on the map using the grid. Use the key to see what the symbols stand for. Two of the barrack blocks are at (2, 0). Can you find them? Go along the bottom or x **axis** first until you find the number 2. Then go up the side or y axis to find the 0.

1. Are the barracks you found barracks a and b, or c and d?
2. Can you work out the grid reference for the headquarters?

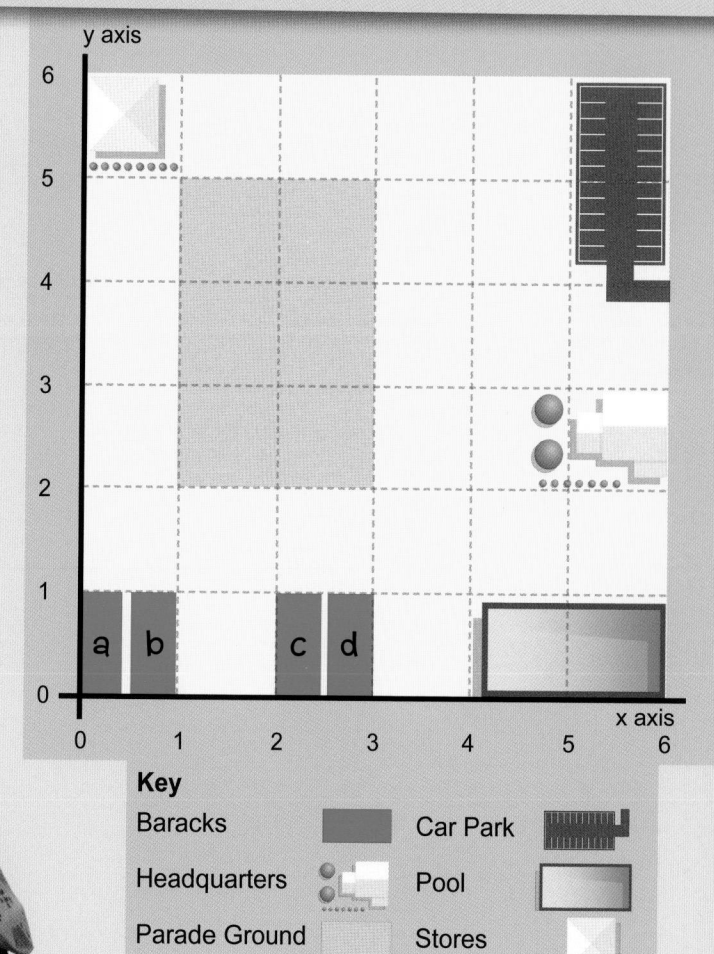

Key

Baracks		Car Park	
Headquarters		Pool	
Parade Ground		Stores	

Do You Know?

You always write the number that belongs to the bottom left hand corner of the square.

Sink the Battleships

You are a navy commander. Your mission is to sink all the battleships on this map. Can you give your crew the correct grid references? If a ship covers more than one square, you need to give the grid reference for all the squares to sink it. Good luck!

Here's one "hit" to get you started — (06, 05).
See if you can get the rest of that ship first.

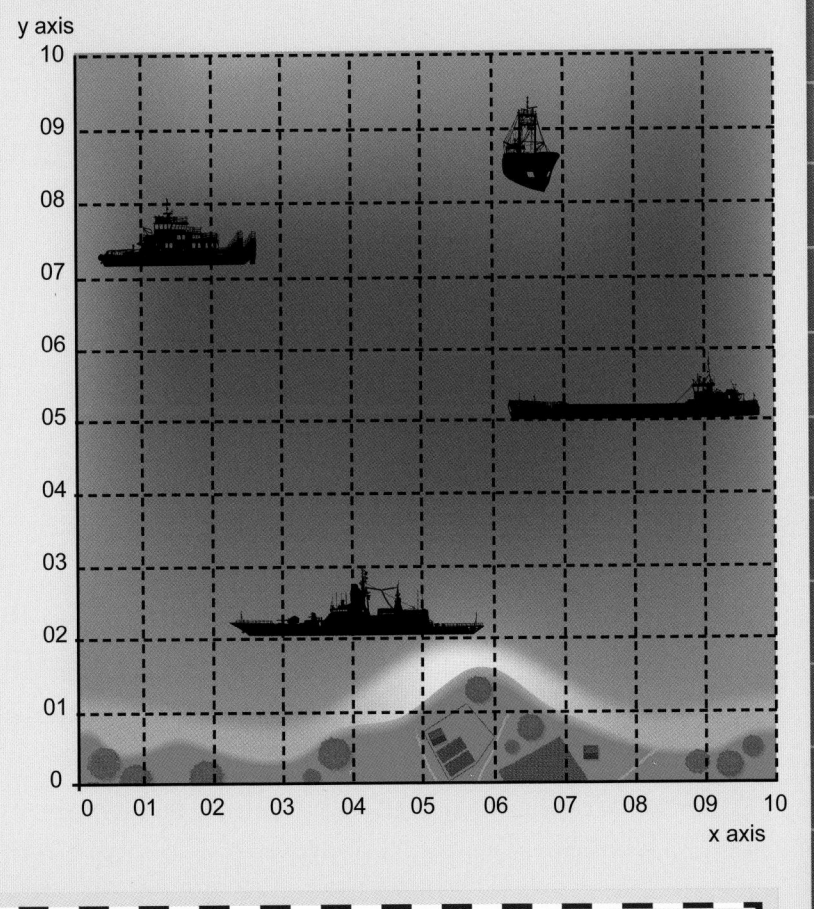

Make Your Own Battleships Game

You can play battleships with a friend. Using graph paper draw two ten square by ten square grids each. Plot your own battleships on one grid. Leave the other grid blank to plot your friend's ships when you find them. Take it in turns to try and sink each other's ships by giving grid references. Mark each hit or miss with an H or an M on your other grid. Mark your opponent's hits on your grid. The first one to sink all the ships wins.

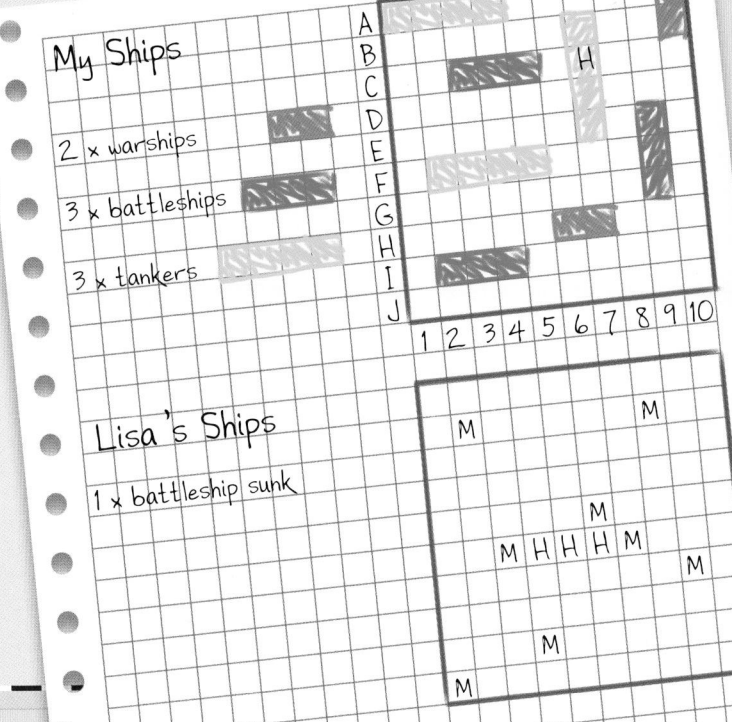

Dividing the World Into Squares

The military use a special grid system to find places on a map. A grid system divides the world up into small squares. The military grid reference system (MGRS) is used by NATO so that all the countries that work together use the same system.

The maps use the Mercator projection so some countries' shapes are a little distorted. The world is divided up into squares. For example, Ireland is at 29U. Find column 29, and then move your finger up the column until you reach square U. The island in that square is Ireland. To find an exact place in Ireland the square can be divided into smaller grid boxes. Using a long reference number that starts 29U you can pinpoint an exact location in Ireland!

Try Your Skills

Look at the map below. Can you tell on what continent grid zones 15T and 15S are.

▼ Can you find the right military grid zone for your house?

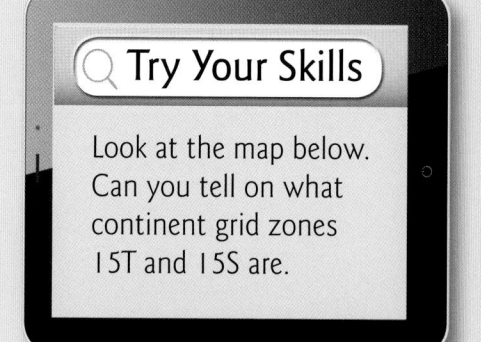

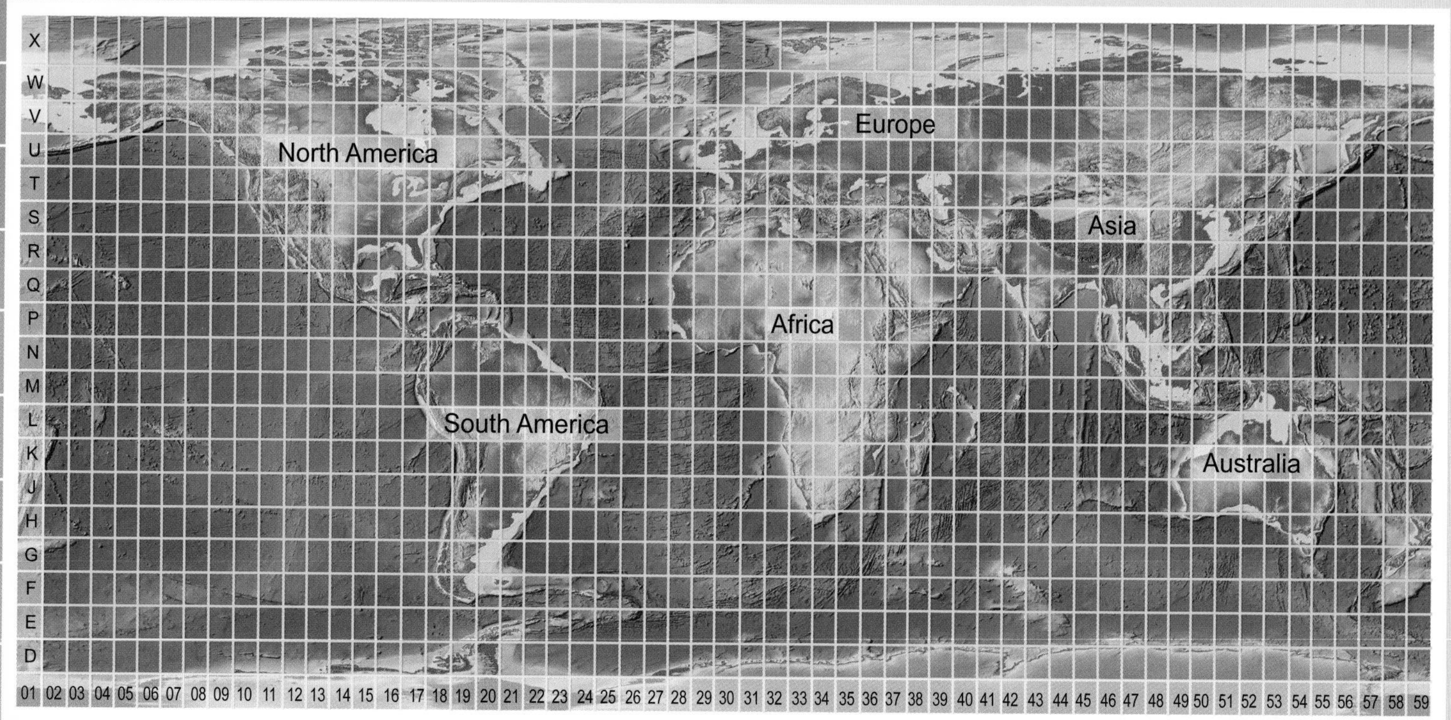

The map on the right is a close-up of the border of grid zones 15T and 15S. A MGRS number is broken up into three parts. The first number and letter (15S) tells us the general area where the location is. The next two letters (VC) gets you to within 62.1 miles (100 km) of the location.

The next four numbers divide the VC square to get to within 0.62 miles (1 km) of the location. If you divide each of those squares into a grid, you can get even more accurate!

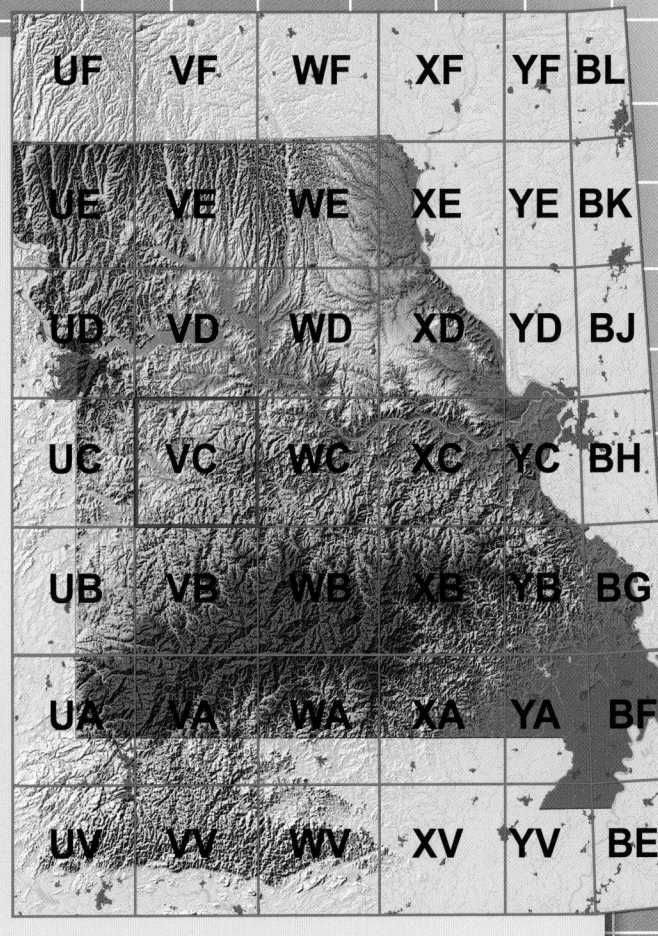

Help The Pilot Find His Way

This map is a close-up view of the grid zone 15SVC. Give the pilot the grid references to get to the locations below. Remember to write the number along the x axis first, followed by the y axis. Start your answer with 15SVC.

1. Airbase
2. Clinton
3. Warsaw

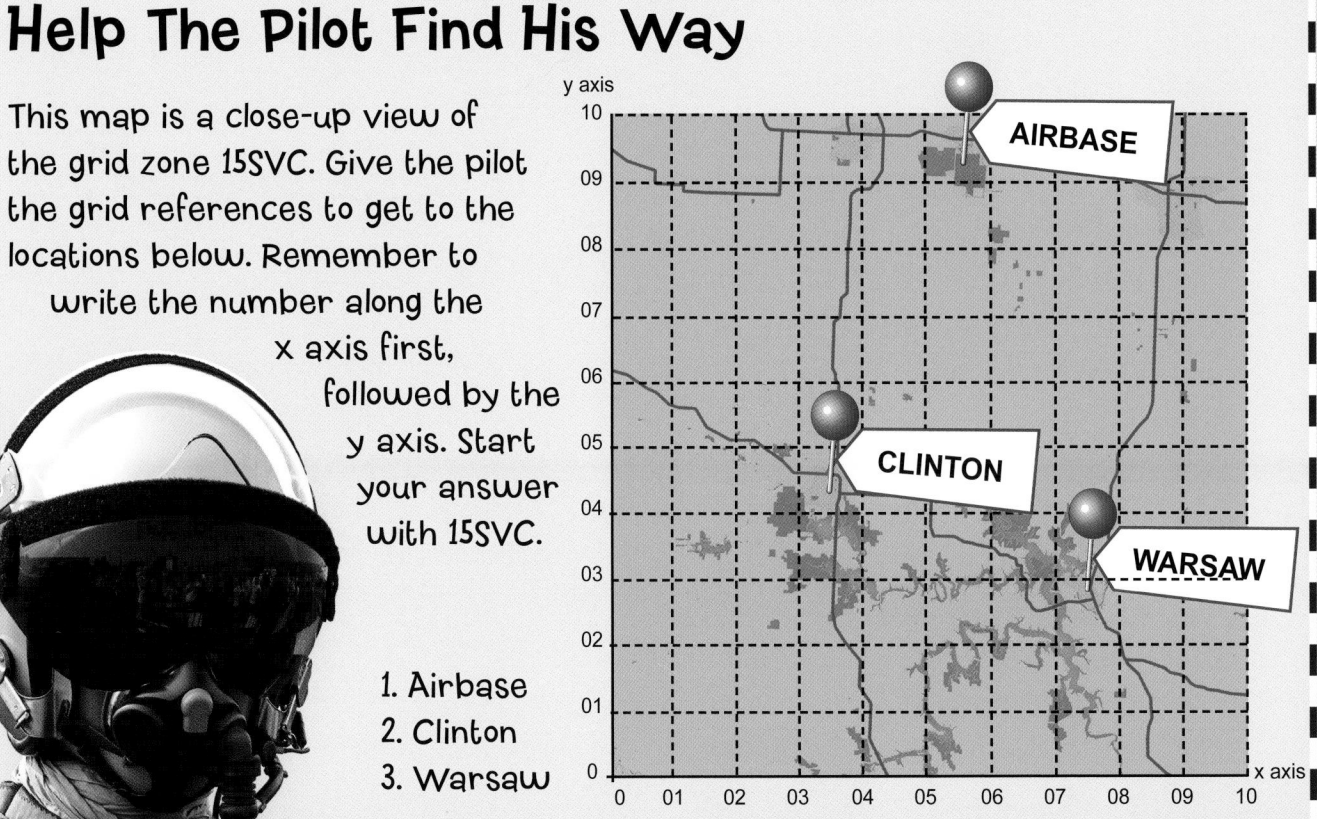

Secret Maps

Maps are used during missions to find targets and escape the enemy, too. Without a map, soldiers can get lost or stumble into enemy territory. During World War II soldiers on secret operations carried maps made of cloth. Why? Cloth maps don't rustle when you open them. They can be hidden inside uniforms, in a seam or inside a collar. They didn't rustle if a soldier was searched. The maps could also be used to mend clothes, filter water, make into a sling or bandage, or even used as a handkerchief!

▲ This silk map was used by Major Oliver Churchill during dangerous undercover missions in Italy during World War II.

During World War II, British Military Intelligence contacted Waddingtons, who made the board game *Monopoly*. They asked them to make board games, packs of cards, and chess sets with cloth maps hidden inside! The games were then sent to prisoner of war camps. A special code was used to tell which country's map was hidden inside which *Monopoly* game, so that it would be sent to a camp in the right area. A period after Marylebone Station meant Italy. A period after Mayfair meant Norway, Sweden, and Germany. A period after Free Parking meant Northern France and Germany!

Do You Know?

A tiny compass and metal file were hidden in the *Monopoly* playing tokens. German, Italian, and French money were mixed into the *Monopoly* money too! Around one-third of the 35,000 prisoners who escaped from the prison camps were helped by a game of *Monopoly*!

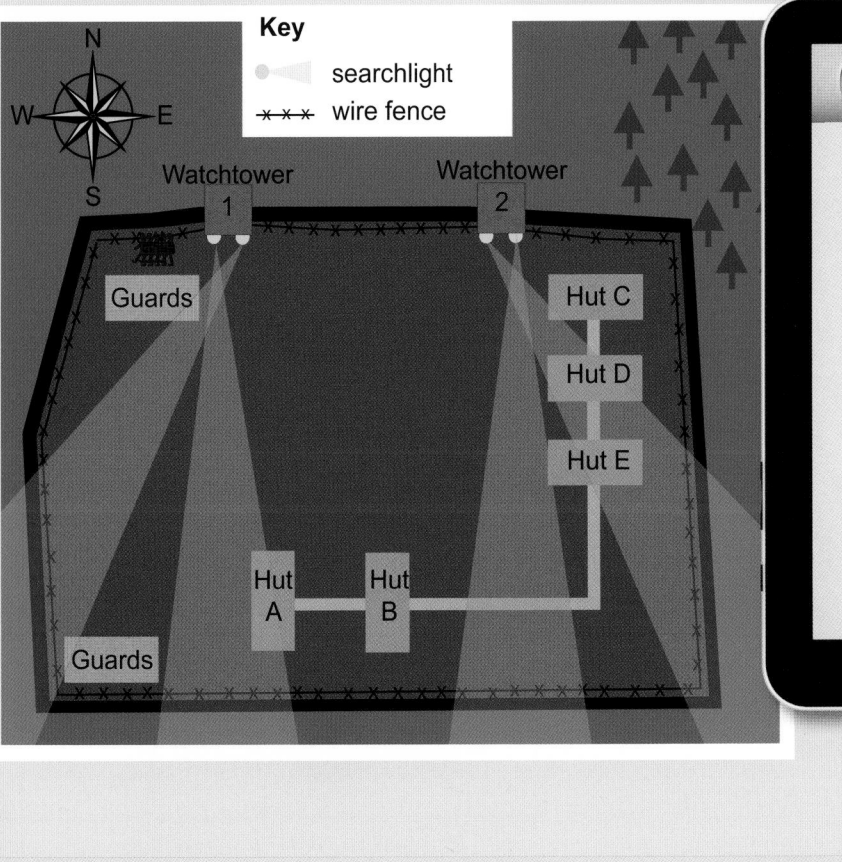

Key

⬤ searchlight

✕✕✕ wire fence

Watchtower 1

Watchtower 2

Guards

Hut A

Hut B

Hut C

Hut D

Hut E

Guards

🔍 Try Your Skills

Using the map, compass, and file, can you escape from this prisoner of war camp?

1. From Hut B, what direction should you head to keep out of the searchlights?

2. How can you cut a hole through the wire fence?

3. Then what direction do you need to head to hide in the woods?

Make Your Own Secret Map

You will need a pencil, some fabric markers, and a square piece of cloth. Sketch your map design onto the cloth with a pencil. You could draw an imaginary place or use a real map to inspire you. Add forests, rivers, and roads. Draw the enemy positions. Label any dangers such as minefields. Put a compass rose on the map too. When you are happy, color it in.

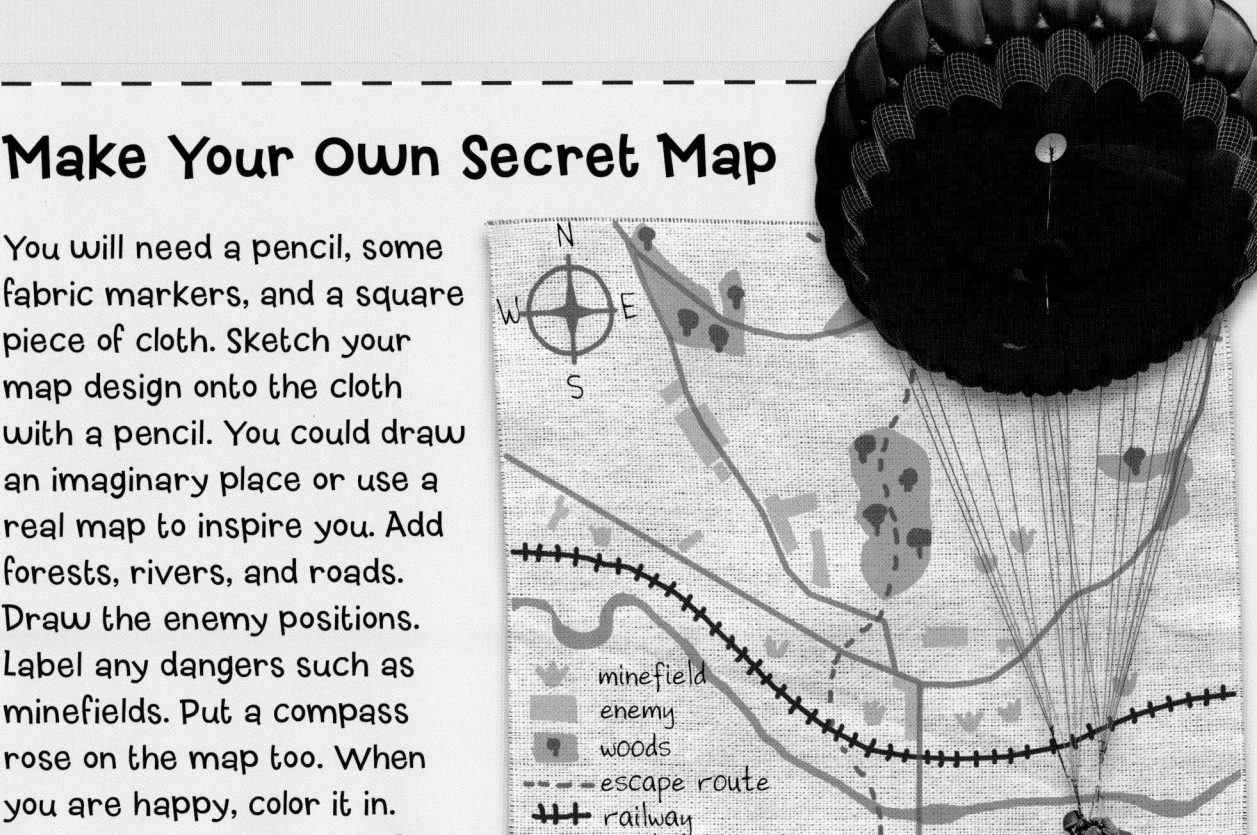

minefield
enemy
woods
escape route
railway
road
river

Different Sizes of Map

A map's **scale** shows you how large the area is that the map covers. The scale lets you work out you how far one place is from another, too. Most maps will have the scale written on them. Maps are not the same size as the places that they show. The scale uses one unit of measurement, for example an inch to represent another unit of measurement, such as a mile. This scale shows 1 inch = 1 mile, 1.58 cm = 1 km.

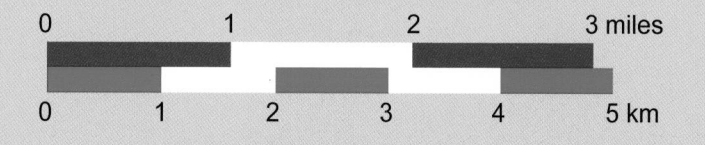

A scale can be written as a **ratio**. The scale 1:10 means that one unit of measurement on a map is the same as 10 units of measurement in real life. So 1 cm on a map would be 10 cm in the real world.

Do You Know?

Military maps use metric measurements, that's cm and km rather than inches and miles.

Q Try Your Skills

You can use the scale to measure distances. Use a piece of string to measure the trails taken by these tanks. Mark the string and measure along the scale. Which tank traveled the farthest?

The military on land usually use a 1:50,000-scale military map. When air, sea, and land troops work together they usually use a 1:250,000 military map. A detailed military city map is usually at 1:12,550. Can you work out which map shows the largest area?

a) 1:50,000 b) 1: 250,000 c) 1:12,550

1)

2)

3)

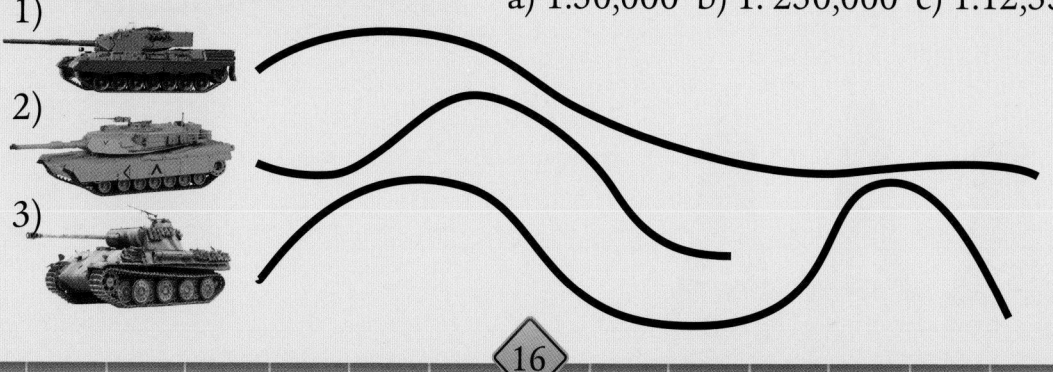

Which Map?

Different scale maps are useful for different military tasks. Look at these three maps of an enemy island. Which map would be best for each of the missions below?

Your Missions

Mission 1.
Plan a raid on Bridgeton barracks. Your team are hiding in the woods nearby.

Mission 2.
Storm the island. Find the safest place to land your boats.

Mission 3.
Intelligence gathering. Find a high place to observe Bridgetown.

a)

Sentinel Mountain

1000 m

Bridgeton

Scale 1 cm = 1 km

0   1   2 km

b)

ENEMY ISLAND

watchtower

rocks

Scale 1 cm = 2 km

0   2   4 km

c)

BRIDGETON

watchtower

barracks

factory

Scale 2 cm = 1 km

0   0.5   1 km

Key

	woods
	towns
	mountains
	marshland
	rivers
	roads
	lake
	beach

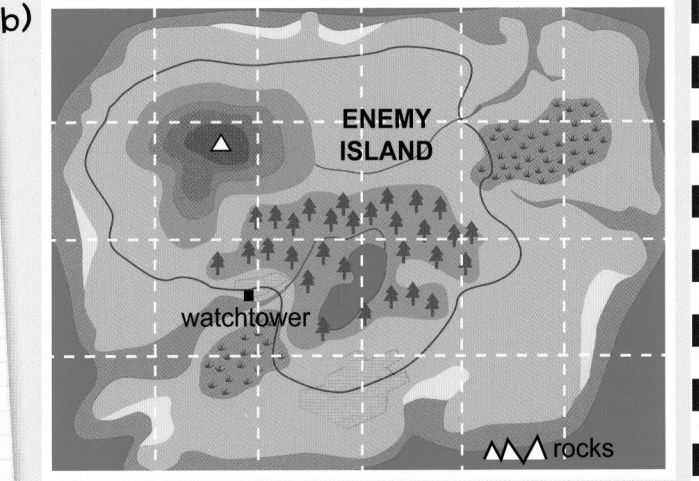

Hitting Targets

Knowing where north, south, east, and west are is useful. But what about all the directions in-between? A compass can give you very accurate directions. The military use compass **bearings** to direct their guns to hit targets accurately. The compass rose is divided into 360 degrees, just like a circle is in math. The military use those degrees to be sure they are firing in exactly the right direction. The military sometimes call a bearing an **azimuth**.

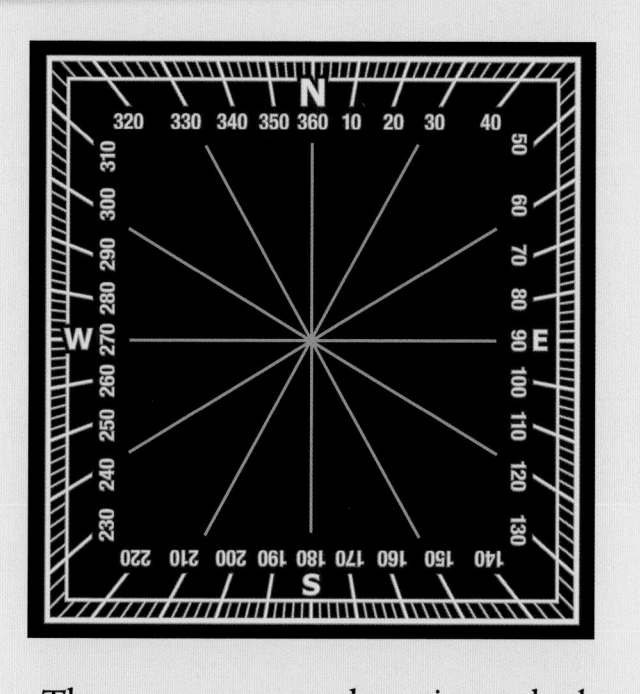

sighting wire

degrees

mils

The compass rose above is marked with the 360 degrees of a compass. You can use this compass to help you with the puzzle on page 19.

The military compass on the right also uses another unit of measure, the mil-radian. They are the black numbers around the outside that go from 0-64. The artillery, tank, and mortar gunnery use these bearings. Mil-radians are called "mils" for short.

Target Practice

You are on a military exercise, where you can practice taking bearings and hitting targets. How many can you hit?

What bearing do you need to hit
1. the sniper?
2. the tank?
3. the big gun?
4. the Chinook helicopter?

Measuring Distance

Knowing the direction of a target is important to make sure you hit it. You also need to know the distance. You need to make sure your shot doesn't fall short or go too far. You have landed on Enemy Island. Can you work out the distance from your gun to these targets? Use a piece of string and measure from the center of the red circles. Then measure the string's length along the scale.

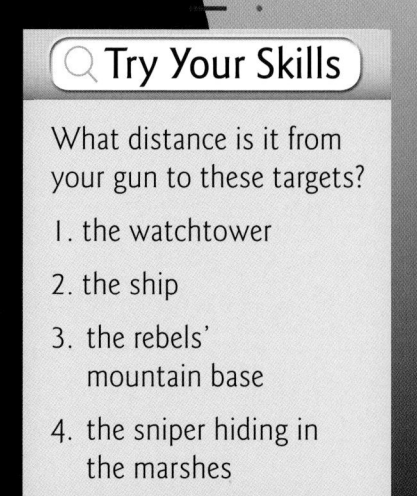

🔍 Try Your Skills

What distance is it from your gun to these targets?

1. the watchtower

2. the ship

3. the rebels' mountain base

4. the sniper hiding in the marshes

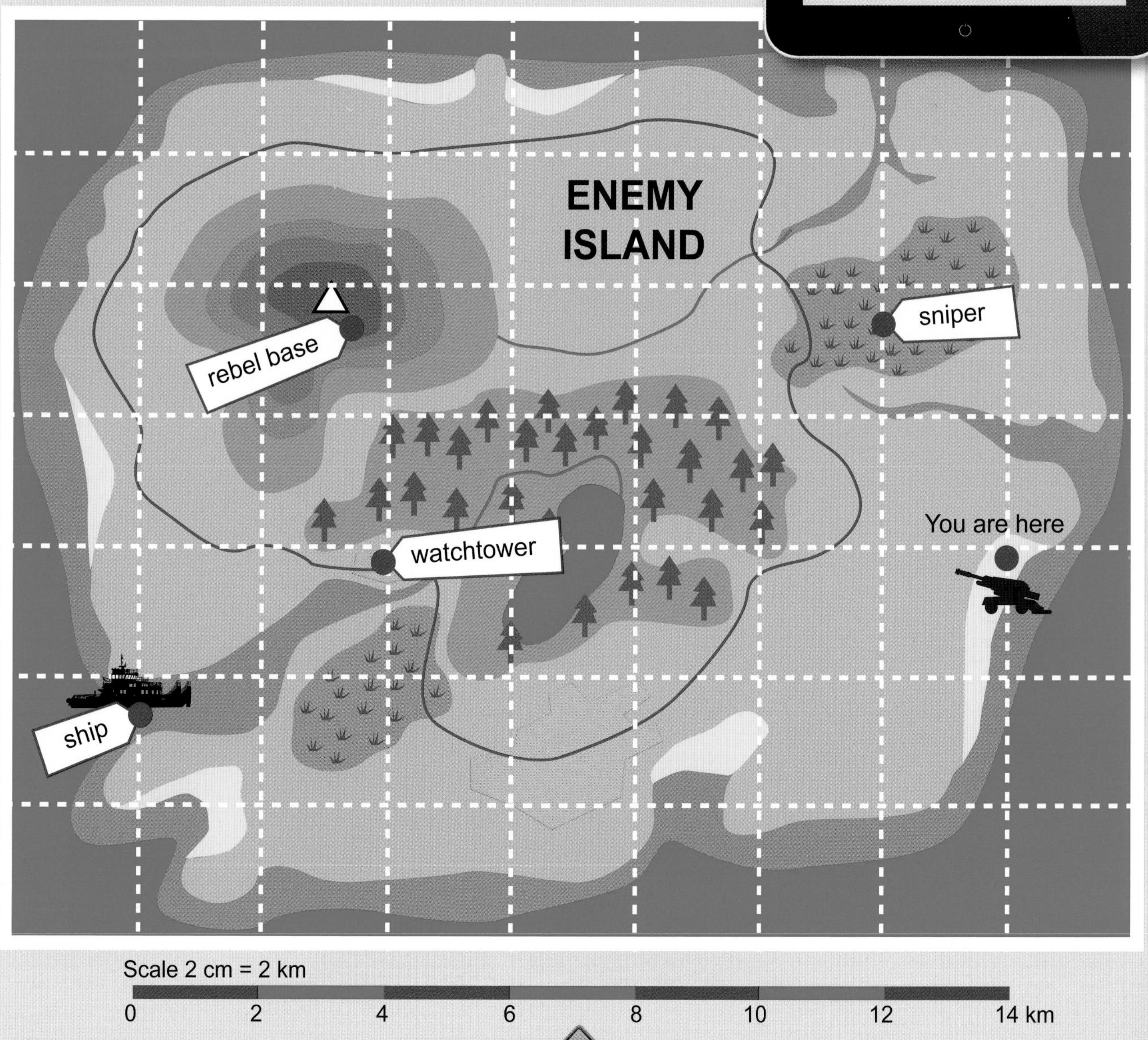

ENEMY ISLAND

sniper

rebel base

You are here

watchtower

ship

Scale 2 cm = 2 km

0   2   4   6   8   10   12   14 km

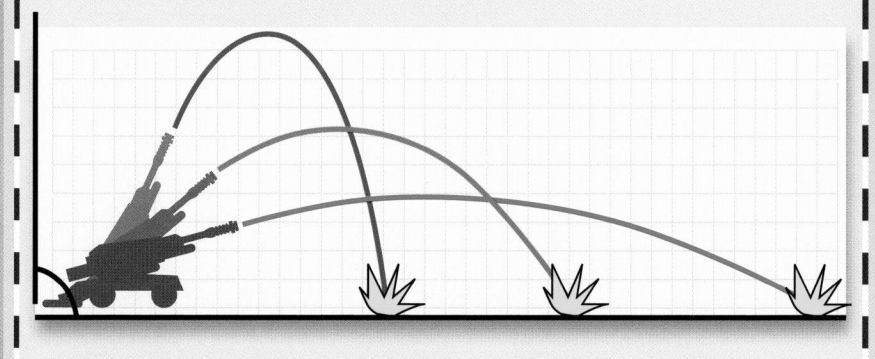

▲ A shell being fired at a steep elevation.

Measuring Arcs

When you shoot a shell out of a mortar, the shell doesn't travel in a straight line. It travels in an arc. Soldiers need to work out how high up in the air they need to aim so that the mortar will hit the target when it comes back down. The angle they need to work out is called the **elevation**. The nearer the target is, the higher the elevation needs to be.

Which one of the targets on Enemy Island would need the highest elevation?

a) the ship b) the sniper c) the watchtower

Do You Know?

A "spotter" watches to see if the mortar shell falls long or short. The gunner can adjust the angle and make a hit next time.

▲ A mortar is a short gun that fires shells. Mortars can be noisy!

Political Maps

Maps don't just tell you where places are. Political maps show country and state boundary lines and leave out **geographic features**. They can show changes in borders that happen over time. During a war, territory is changing hands all the time. Up-to-date maps are needed to keep track of which areas have fallen into enemy hands. They are useful to help plan your action, too.

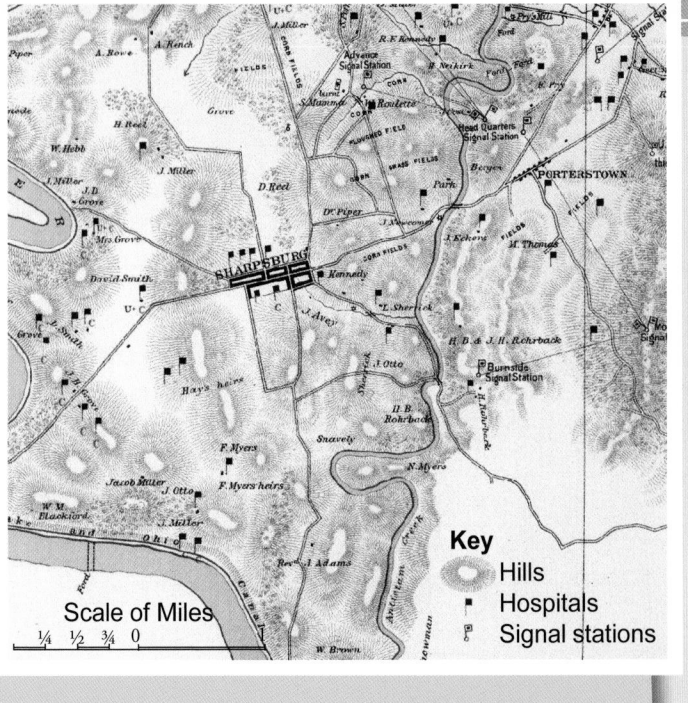

Key
- Hills
- Hospitals
- Signal stations

Scale of Miles
¼ ½ ¾ 0

▲ This map is of the American Civil War Battle of Antietam. The fields, hills, hospitals, and signal stations are marked to help plan the attacks.

Make Your Own Battle Map

During battles, military leaders use a map showing the area of land being fought over. The map shows the troops and equipment available. Nowadays this mapping is done on a computer. In previous wars, a paper map and movable pieces were used to show how a battle was progressing. The pieces would be moved about the map using long sticks, a little like a board game!

1. Draw a big map of a battlefield on some paper.

2. Draw tanks, soldiers, aircraft, and ships onto small pieces of card. Remember to draw your side and the enemy side. Color them in different colors.

3. Move the cards around the map as the battle starts.

4. It's up to you to manage the battle and make sure your side wins!

War and Maps

Look at these two maps of Europe. The map at the top shows the countries' borders as they are now. The map at the bottom shows the borders during World War II after Germany had invaded many of its neighbors. The color of a country on the map changed to the same color as Germany once it had been invaded.

Can you work out the answers to these questions?

1. What color was Germany?

2. Was Germany country a, b, or c on Map 1?

3. The light shade of Germany's color shows where there is fighting taking place. Do you think fighting is in area d, e, or f?

Do You Know?

Can you find out which country was the green one surrounded by blue countries? Look at an atlas or online map to help you.

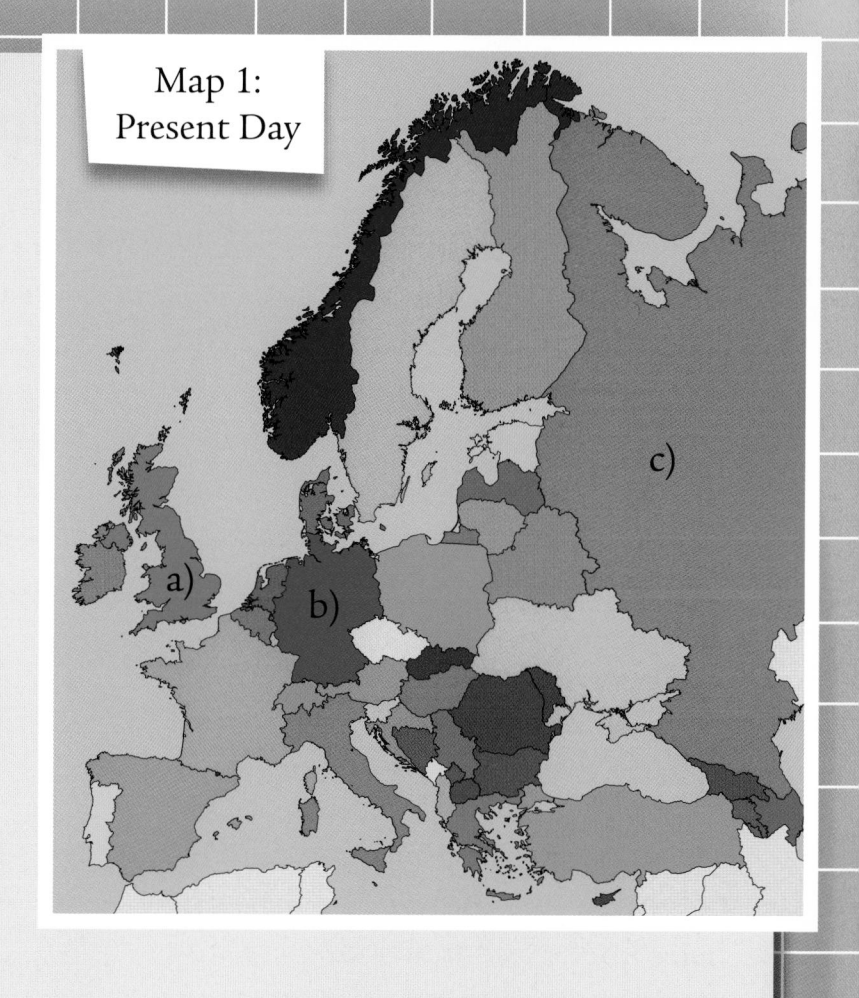

Map 1:
Present Day

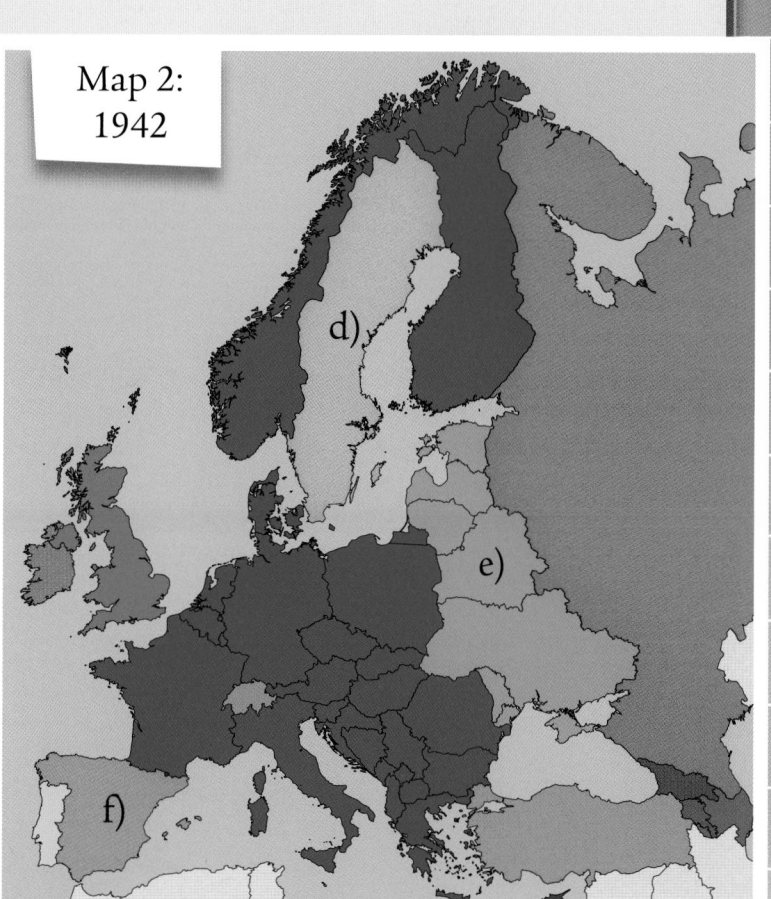

Map 2:
1942

Mapping Hills and Valleys

The type of **terrain** that the military operate on is important. Mountain ranges are hard to go across on foot. Marshland may be impossible to cross in a tank. Mountains may get in the way of low-flying aircraft. **Topographical** maps show the land in detail. They show all the man-made and natural features of an area. They usually show the height of the terrain using **contour lines**. Contour lines link areas that are the same height.

250 ft

150 ft

100 ft

50 ft

During the Vietnam War "the Rockpile" below, was used as a US Marines' look-out post and base for two years. It could only be reached by helicopter. A small wooden landing platform was built on the top of the mountain. All supplies and troops were brought to the Rockpile in this way. The platform was so small the helicopter could only touch down with one wheel! The pilots had to be very skillful.

Do You Know?

Contour lines can tell you at a glance how easy a mountain would be to climb. If contour lines are close together, the slope is steep. If they are far apart, the slope is shallow.

The Rockpile is called Thon Khe Tri in Vietnamese.

▼ A helicopter trying to land on the small wooden platform during the Vietnam War.

Contour Map of The Rockpile

The Rockpile was an important piece of territory during the Vietnam war. The Marines had a good view of the area to search for any signs of enemy movement. The topographical map below shows the area around the Rockpile. Here are some descriptions of the Rockpile. Can you work out if the Rockpile is a, b, c, or d?

- The Rockpile is surrounded by flat land
- There is a clear view over five different valleys from the top of the Rockpile
- The Rockpile has steep sides
- The road runs to the southeast of the Rockpile.
- The Rockpile is almost circular in shape
- Rivers run to the north and the south of the Rockpile

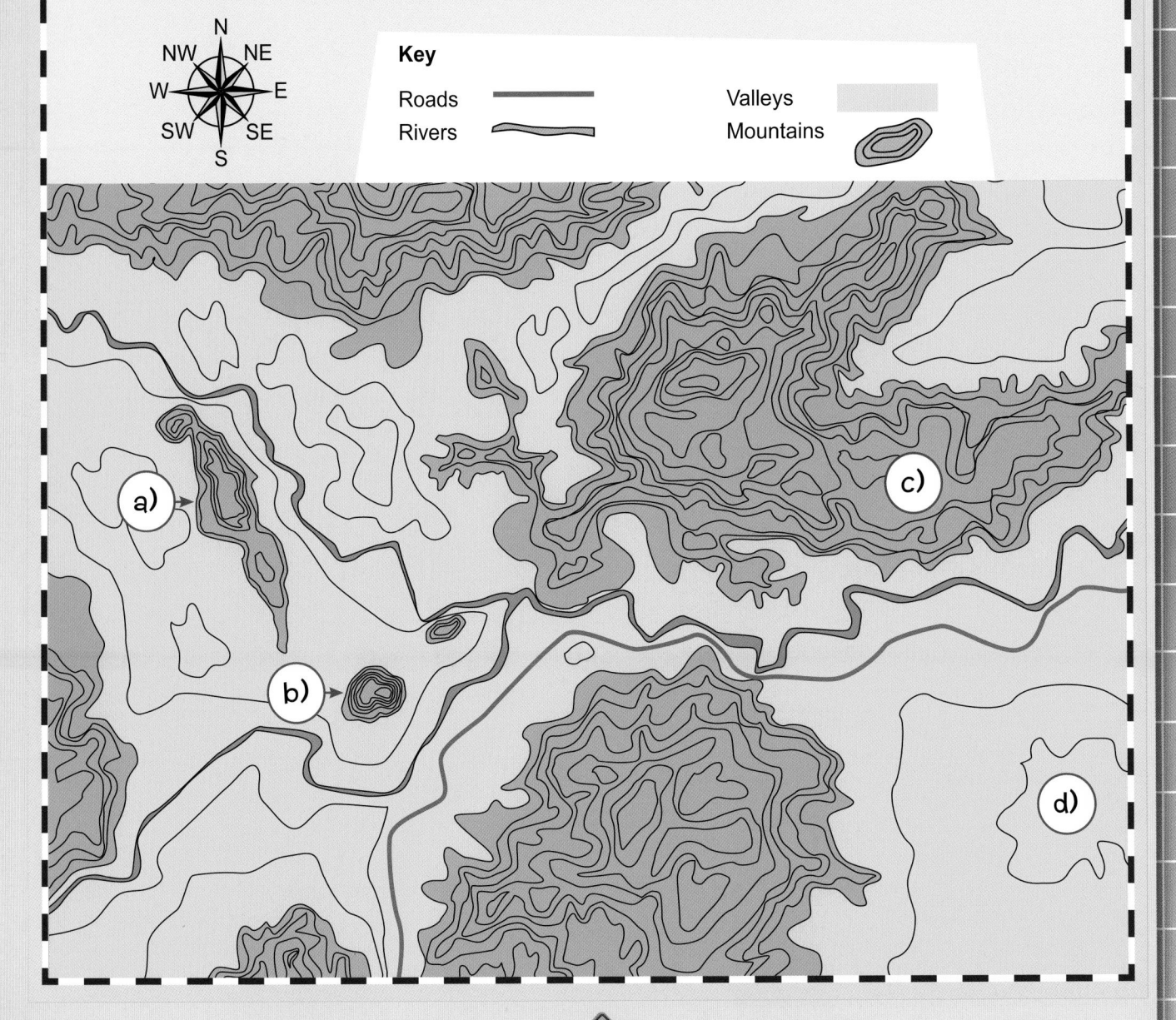

Key

Roads ——————

Rivers 〜〜〜

Valleys

Mountains

Global Positioning Systems

A global positioning system (**GPS** for short) is a system of **satellites** and **receivers** which can tell you where you are and give you directions to other places. GPS is what a car's satellite navigation uses to know its position and plan routes. GPS was developed by the military. Today, GPS is carried by ground soldiers, attached to vehicles, warships, and aircraft in combat zones.

▲ a satellite

GPS helps ground troops cross terrain such as large deserts that have no landmarks. GPS is also useful when soldiers can't see where they are going, such as during a sand storm. In the future every soldier may wear a GPS device sewn into their uniforms so that field commanders can track their movements.

▼ A platoon leader on patrol in Afghanistan checks his location using a handheld GPS.

Do You Know?

Once a target has been identified, GPS helps bombers aim their strikes. The UK's Royal Air Force used GPS for this attack on a Libyan weapons store.

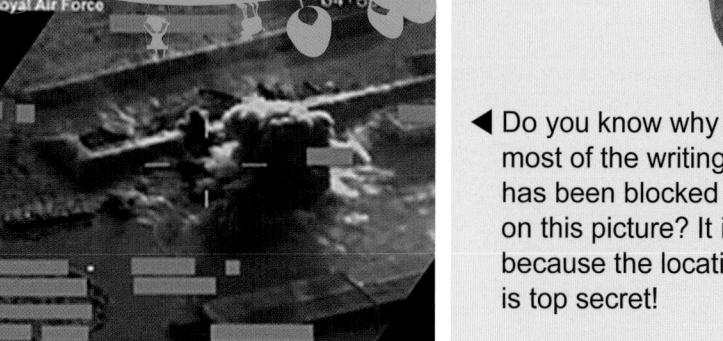

Royal Air Force

◀ Do you know why most of the writing has been blocked out on this picture? It is because the location is top secret!

How GPS Works

Satellites travel around the Earth twice a day transmitting radio signals. GPS receivers pick up the signals. GPS works using **trilateration**. "Tri" means "three." The GPS receiver has to know the location of at least three satellites above you and the distance between you and each of those satellites. Trilateration works kind of like this:

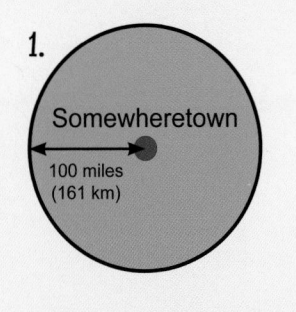

1.

Somewheretown

100 miles
(161 km)

Imagine you are totally lost and someone tells you that you are 100 miles (161 km) from Somewheretown. You know that you are somewhere within a circle with a 100 mile (161 km) radius of Somewheretown.

2.

Somewheretown

point a

Elsewhere

60 miles
(97 km)

point b

The next person you meet tells you that you are 60 miles (97 km) from Elsewhere. Now you have two circles that cross each other. To be exactly 60 miles (97 km) from Elsewhere, AND 100 miles (161 km) from Somewheretown you must be at either point a, or point b.

3.

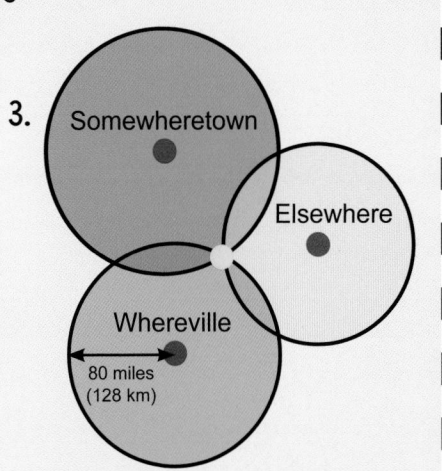

Somewheretown

Elsewhere

Whereville

80 miles
(128 km)

When a third person tells you that you are 80 miles (128 km) from Whereville, you know exactly where you are. That circle will only cross one of those points.

◯ You are at Hometown

🔍 Try Your Skills

Can you set a trilateration puzzle for a friend? Find three places on a map that would form a triangle if you drew lines between them. Give your friend the distance you are from the three places and see if they can work out your location. Use a pair of compasses to draw the circles on tracing paper or **acetate** over the map.

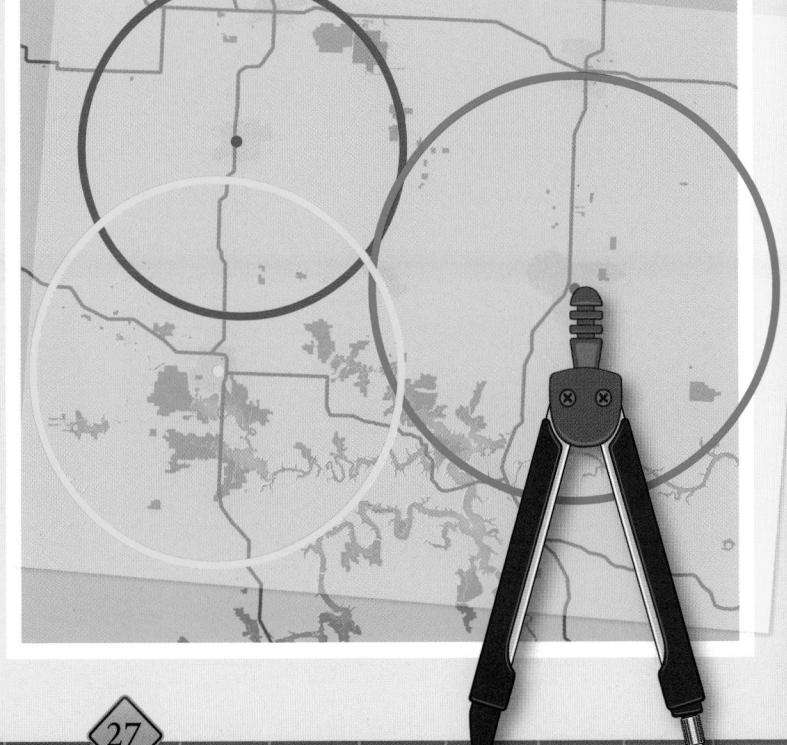

Layers of Information

Military forces use Geographic Information Systems (**GIS**) to give them information about an area. GIS is computer **software** that can link an area's map with other information about that area. GIS uses layers. One layer could show the roads and paths, another could show the average rainfall, or where people live, perhaps. GIS is very useful when planning military operations.

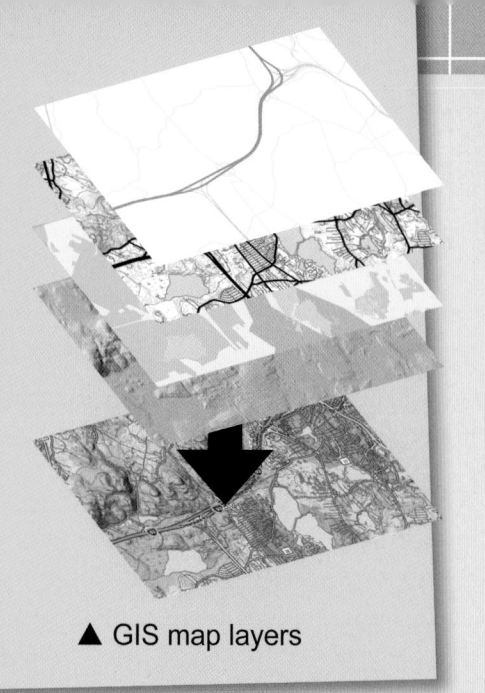

▲ GIS map layers

Some weapons need to be able to see their targets to work. The military use GIS to make sure there are no mountains in between them and their targets. GIS can be programmed to show a real-time map of which troops and equipment are available in an area too.

Military engineers build their own bases using GIS maps to help them. When they plan the buildings they can look at the landscape from different angles. They can look for information about areas of rock, or check for pipes and cables where they may have to dig.

▲ GIS maps used by the US Corps of Engineers in Wiesbaden, Germany to build a new base.

Do You Know?

GIS systems can help military emergency prepared teams. GIS can help work out the path of a hurricane, for example.

Make Your Own Layer Map

Try making you own layered GIS-style map with different information about an area. The base map shows the terrain, such as the hills and valleys. Decide what information the other layers should have on them. Perhaps your troops will need to know where the widest roads are, so they can bring in large vehicles. Or perhaps they need to know if there are any hostile areas? Maybe they need to hide in trees and bushes?

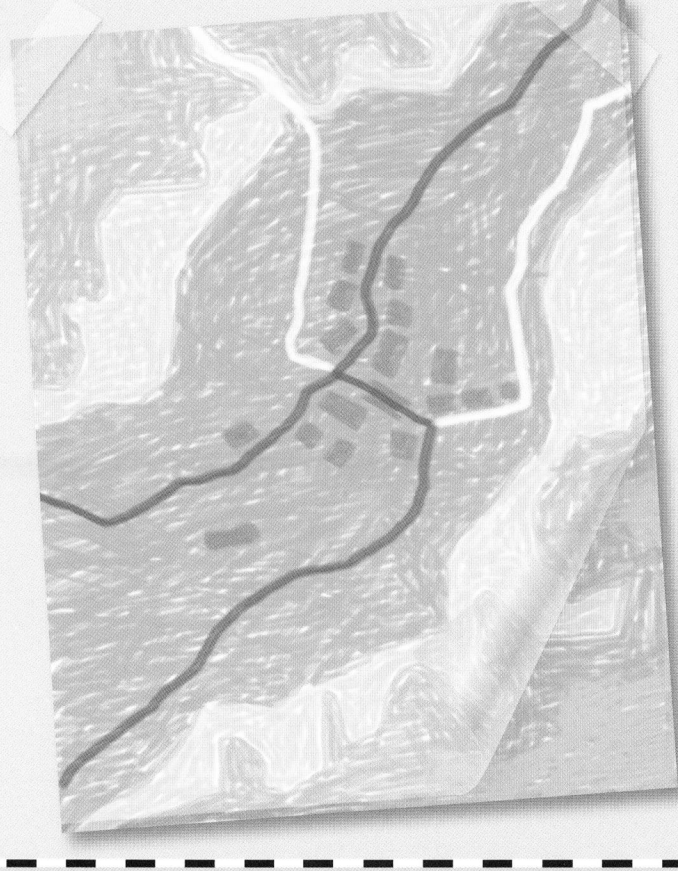

1. Draw your base map on some paper.

2. Lay a sheet of acetate over the base map and tape it down so it keeps still. Draw on your next layer of information, such as the roads.

3. You can overlay as many sheets of acetate as you might need.

Glossary

acetate (A-seh-tayt)
A transparent sheet which can
be drawn on.

axis (AK-sus)
A number line (as an x-axis or a
y-axis) along which coordinates
are measured.

azimuth (AZ-muth)
Horizontal direction of an object from
a fixed point expressed as an angle.

bearings (BER-ingz)
The positions or directions of one
point with respect to another or to
the compass.

cardinal directions
(KAHRD-nul dih-REK-shunz)
One of the four principal points of
the compass: north, south, east, west.

compass rose (KUM-pus ROHZ)
A drawing on a map
showing directions.

contour lines (KON-toor LYNZ)
Lines on a map connecting
points with the same elevation
on a land surface.

elevation (eh-luh-VAY-shun)
The height to which something
is raised.

geographic features
(jee-uh-GRA-fik FEE-churz)
Components of the earth, either
natural such as terrain and bodies
of water, or man-made such as
human settlements, bridges and
other constructions.

GIS (JEE-EYE-ES)
GIS is short for Geographic
Information Systems. GIS uses
hardware and software to map
and analyze geographic data.

GPS (JEE-PEE-ES)
GPS is short for global positioning
system. GPS devices tell you your
exact position by using information
from orbiting satellites.

grid reference
(GRID REH-frens)
A point on a map defined by two sets
of numbers or letters.

north magnetic pole
(NORTH mag-NEH-tik POHL)
The direction of the earth's
magnetic pole.

projections
(pruh-JEK-shunz)
A method of showing a curved surface
on a flat one.

ratio (RAY-shoh)
The relationship in quantity, amount, or size between things.

receivers (rih-SEE-verz)
Equipment for receiving radio or television signals.

satellites (SA-tih-lyts)
Man-made objects orbiting around the earth, moon, or another planet transmitting scientific information to earth or used for communication.

scale (SKAYL)
Size in comparison.

software (SOFT-wayr)
The programs and related information used by a computer.

topographical
(tah-puh-GRA-fih-kul)
Showing the heights and depths of the features of a place.

trilateration
(try-la-tuh-RAY-shun)
A method of determining position by using the relative positions of three or more points.

Read More

Colson, Rob. *Tanks and Military Vehicles*. New York: PowerKids Press, 2013.

Gray, Leon. *How Does GPS Work?* New York: Gareth Stevens, 2014.

Rodger, Ellen. *Atlas and Globe Skills*. St Catharines, Ontario: Crabtree Publishing Company, 2013.

Due to the changing nature of Internet links, PowerKids Press has developed an online list of websites related to the subject of this book. This site is updated regularly. Please use this link to access the list:

www.powerkidslinks.com/fwms/mili/

Index

Answers

page 6
1. 3, 2. 3, 3. 1, 4. 2
page 7
1. d, 2. a, 3. i, 4. b, 5. c, 6. j,
7. e, 8. h, .9 g, 10. f
page 8
1. south, 2. west, 3. north,
4. north
page 9
1. north, 2. 90°, 3. north
4. south, 5. west
page 10
1. c and d, 2. (5, 2)

page 11
(06, 08) (06, 09), (06, 05)
(07, 05) (08, 05) (09, 05),
(0, 07) (01, 07) (02, 07),
(02, 02) (03, 02) (04, 02)
(05, 02)
page 13
Try Your Skills
North America
1. 15S VC 0509; 2. 15S VC
0304; 3. 15S VC 0702
page 15
1. north, 2. with the file,
3. east

page 16
Try Your Skills
tank 1, b)
page 17
1. c, 2. b, 3. a
page 19
1. 300°, 2. 30°, 3. 360°,
4. 330°
page 20
1. watchtower 10 km,
2. ship 14 km, 3. top of
mountain 11 km,
4. sniper 4 km

page 21
b) the sniper
page 23
1. blue, 2. b, 3. e
Do you know?
Switzerland

page 25
Rockpile is b